This Book Belongs to

_____

_____

_____

_____

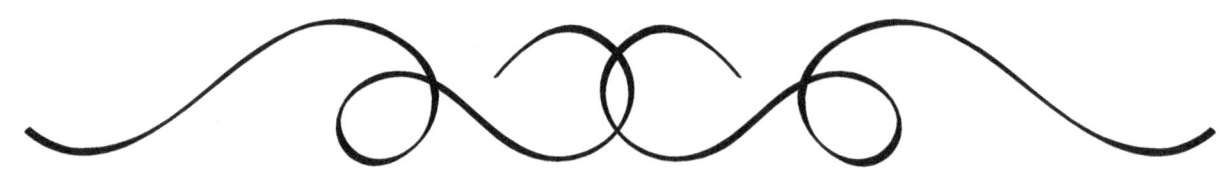

About This Coloring Book

This Coloring Book is for boys and girls. This book is great fun and inspiring to learn and Filled with many types of activities it will stimulate the brain, inspire creativity, and develop skills.

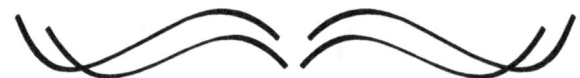

COPYRIGHT DISCLAIMER

All rights reserved. This book or any portion thereof may not be reproduced or used in any manner whatsoever without the express written permission of the publisher. You may scan and print the images for personal use so you can color them multiple times or print them on a different type of paper. Do not sell any colored images from this book for profit.

Note: *The Book has been designed using Free and Premium resources from 123rf, Creative Fabrica, Freepik.*

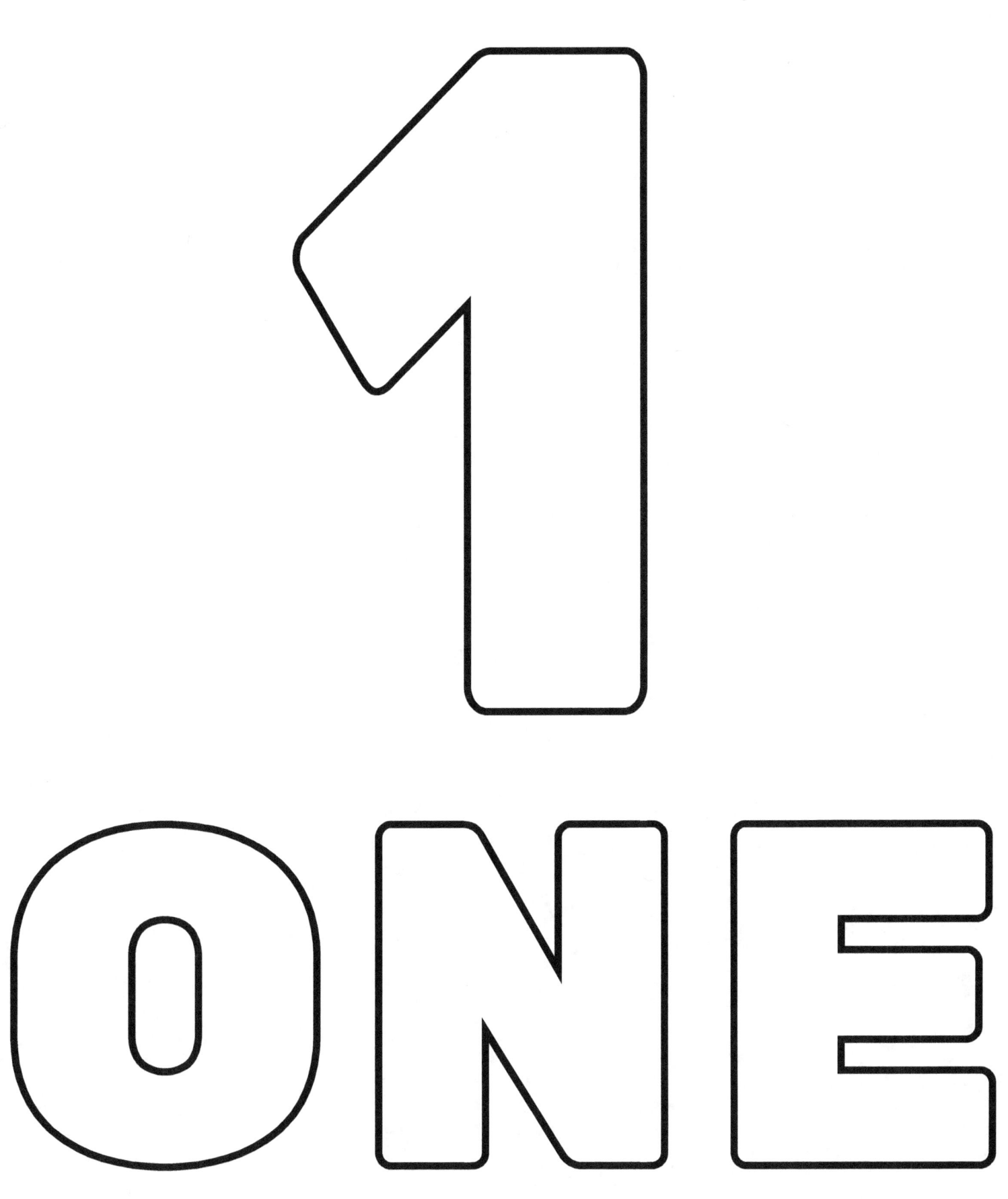

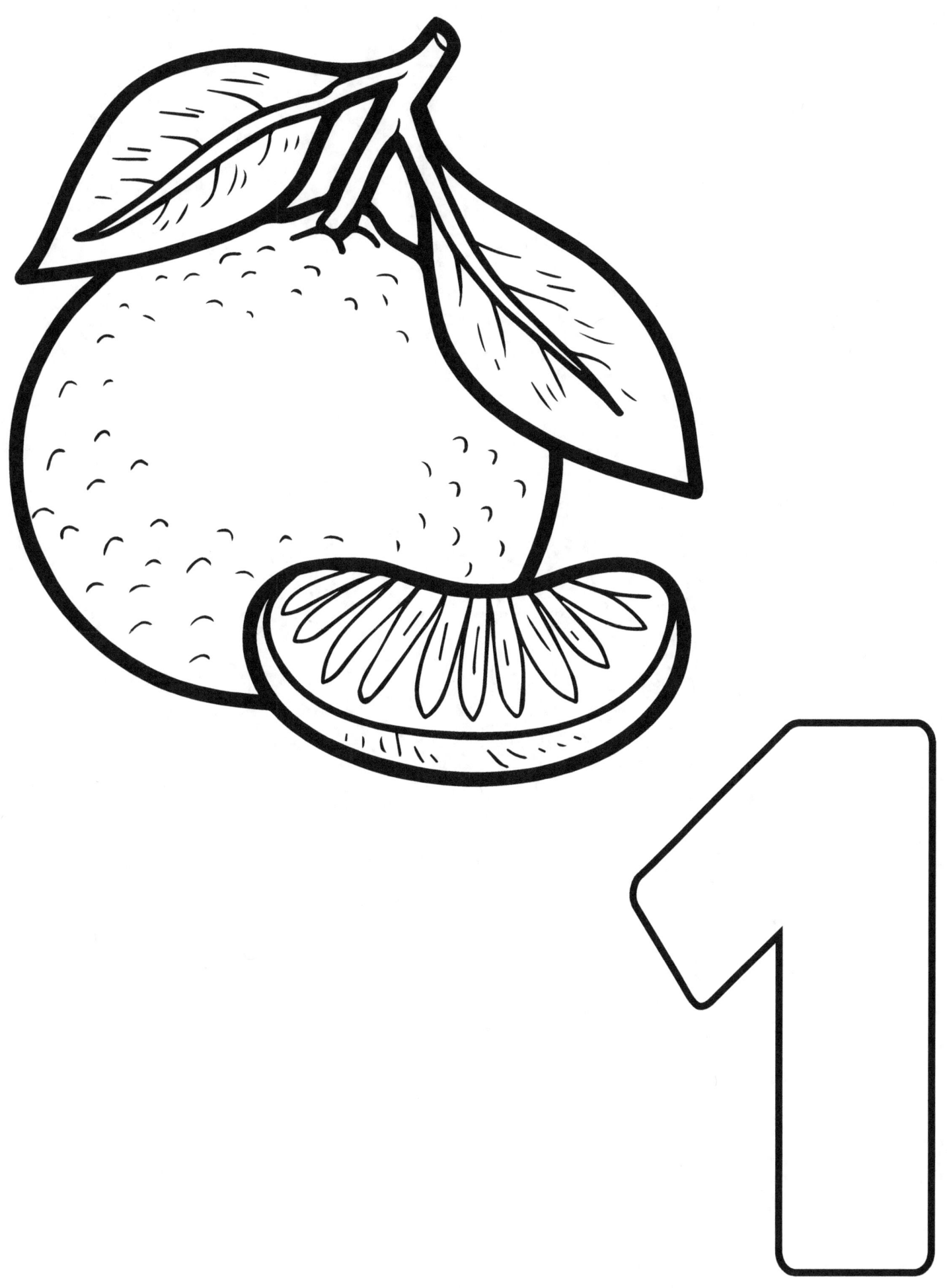

2
TWO

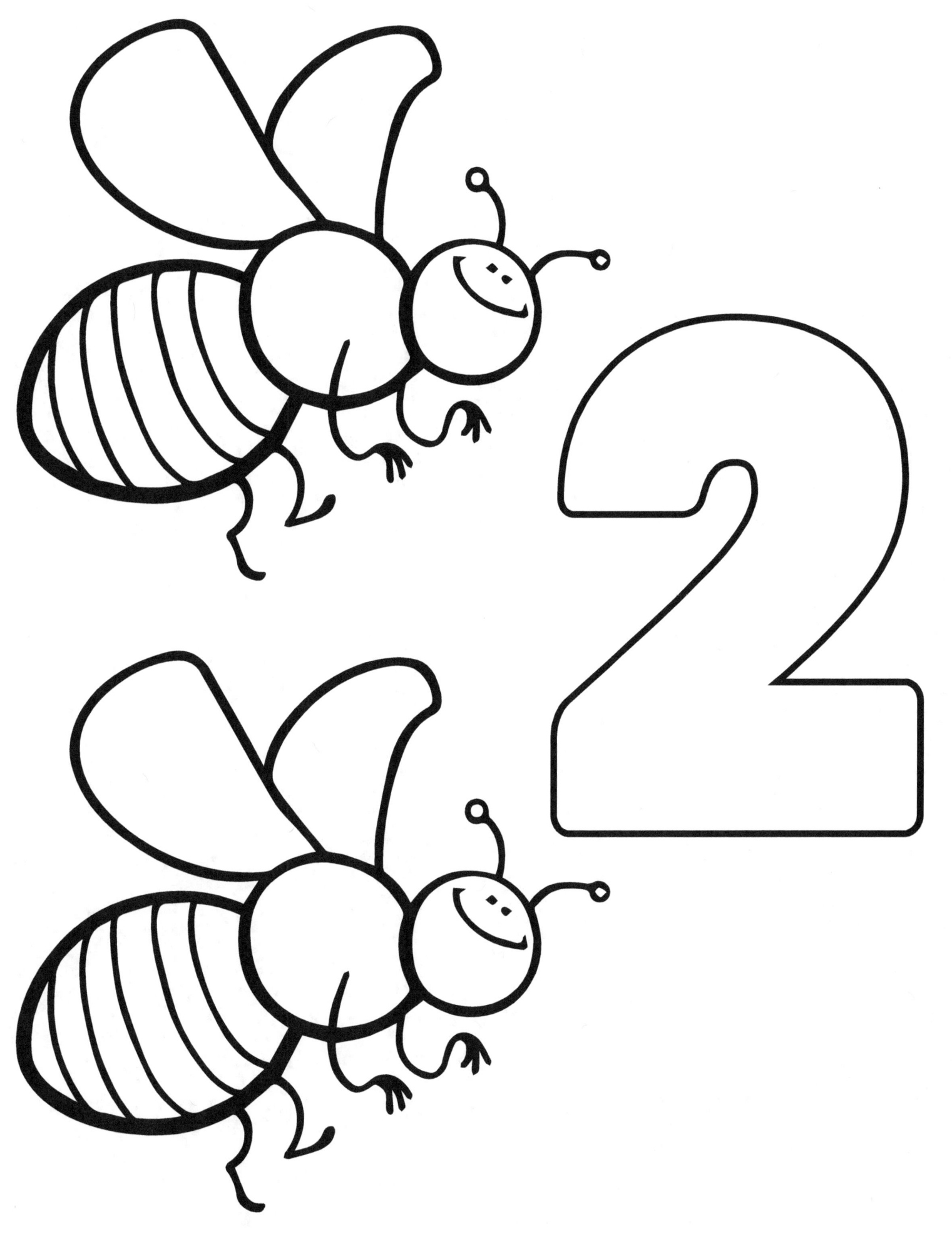

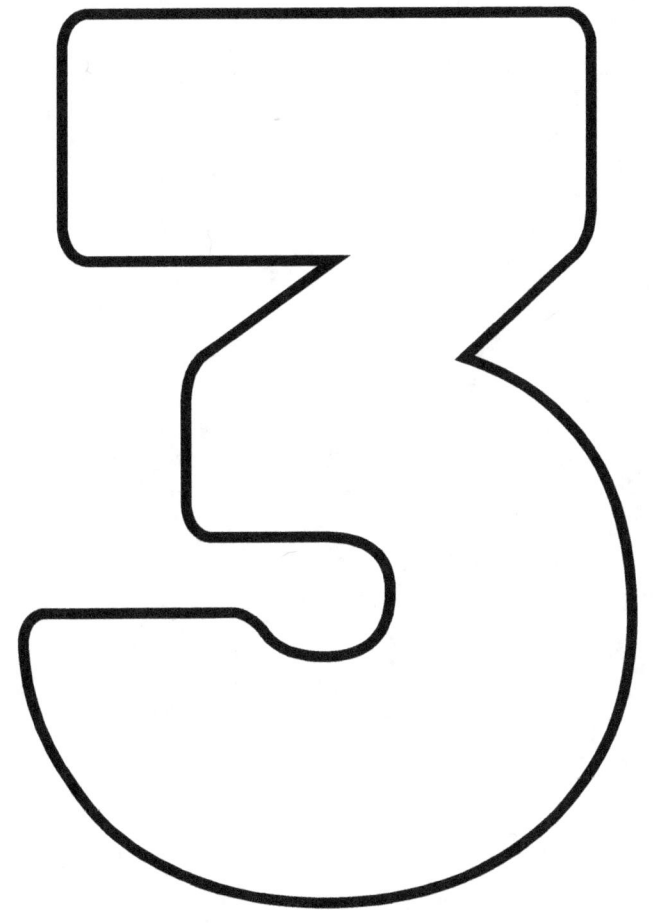

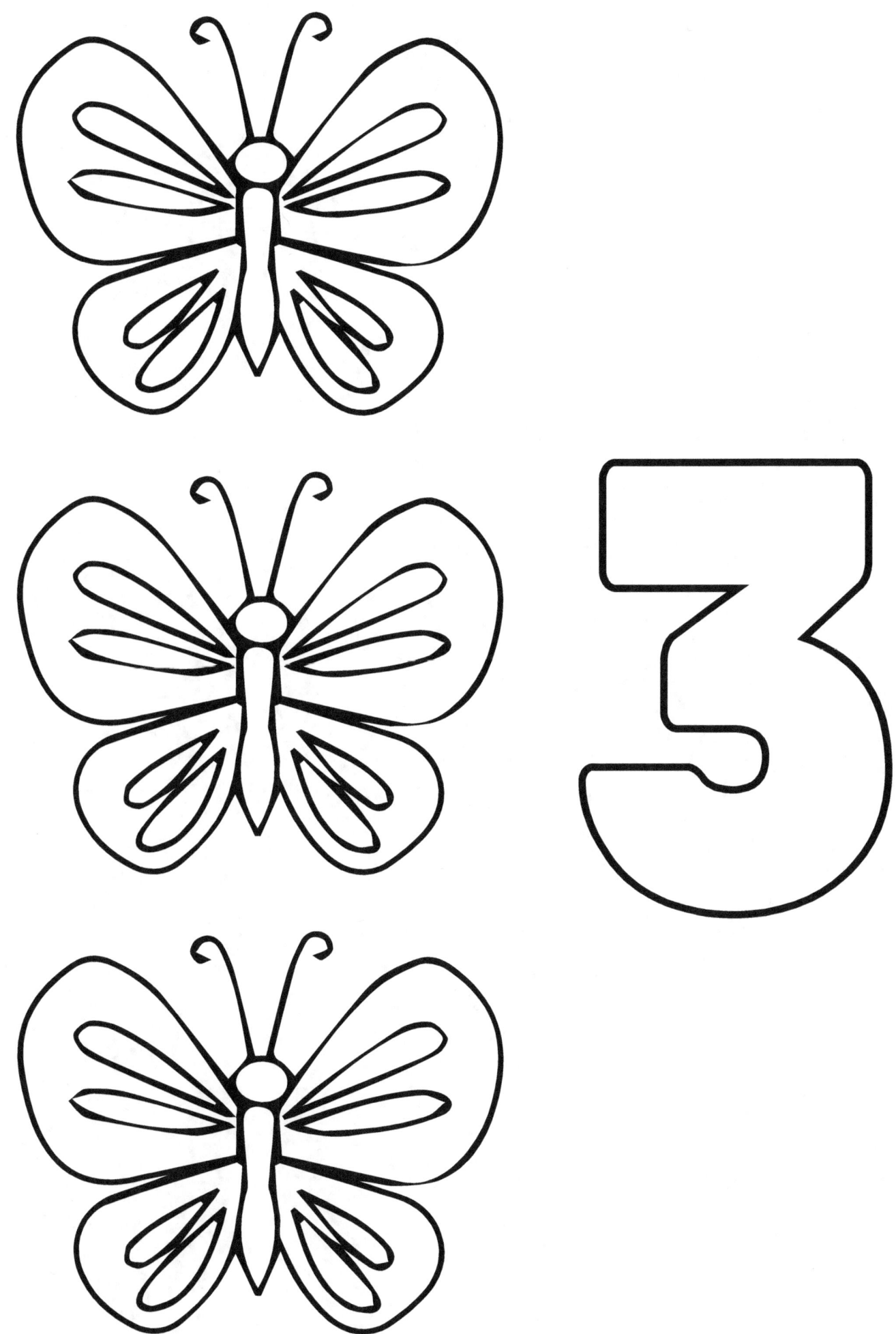

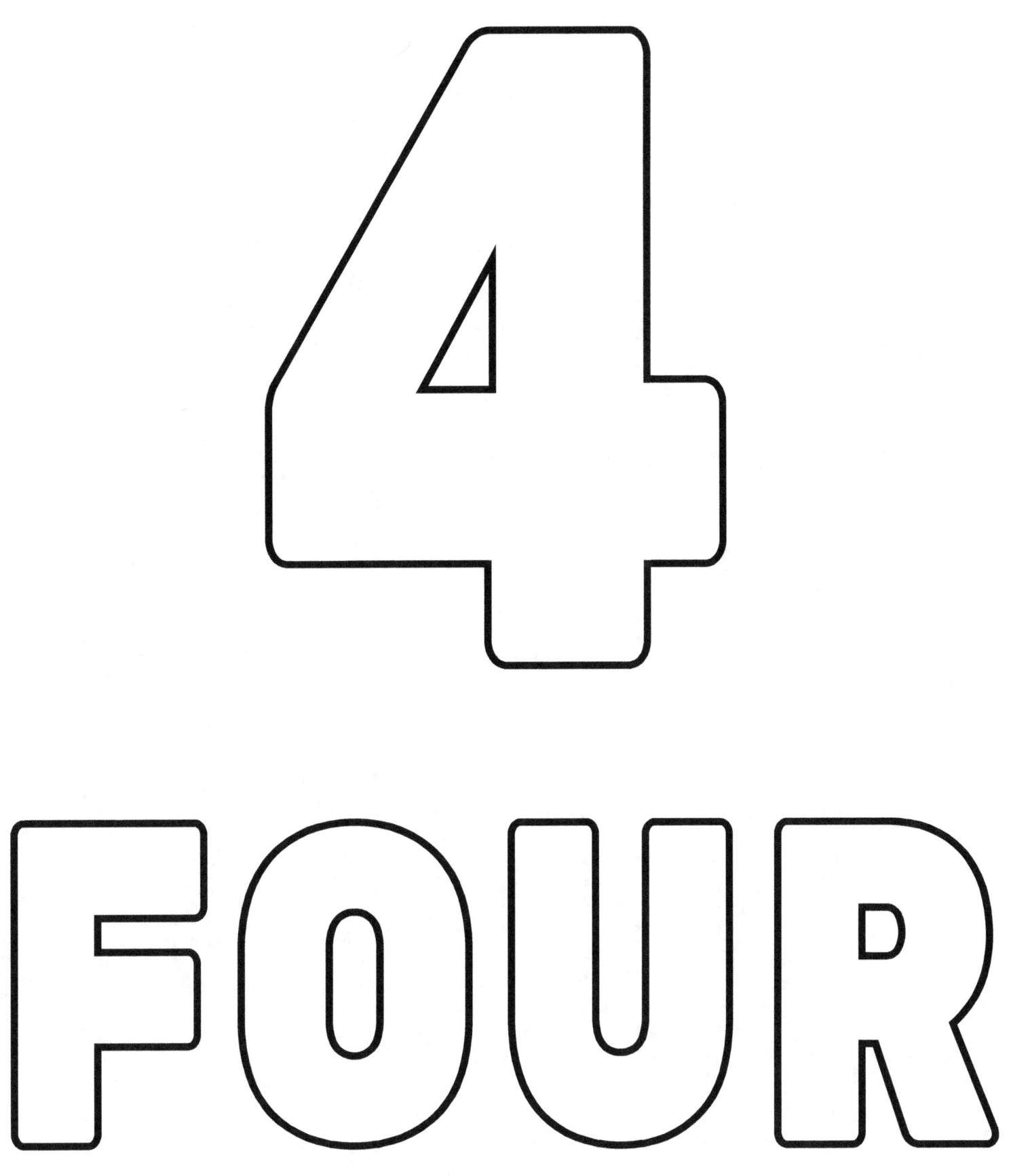

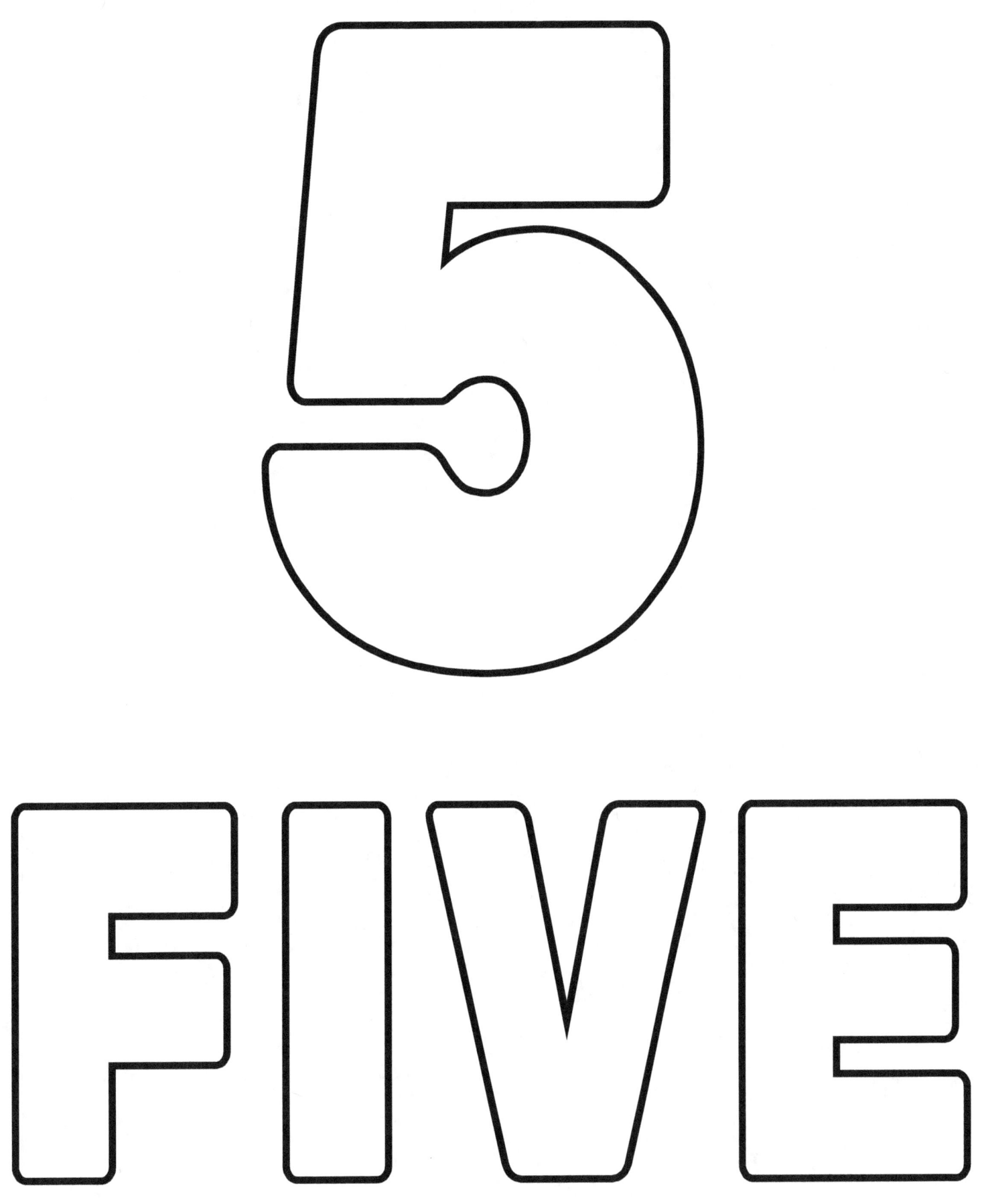

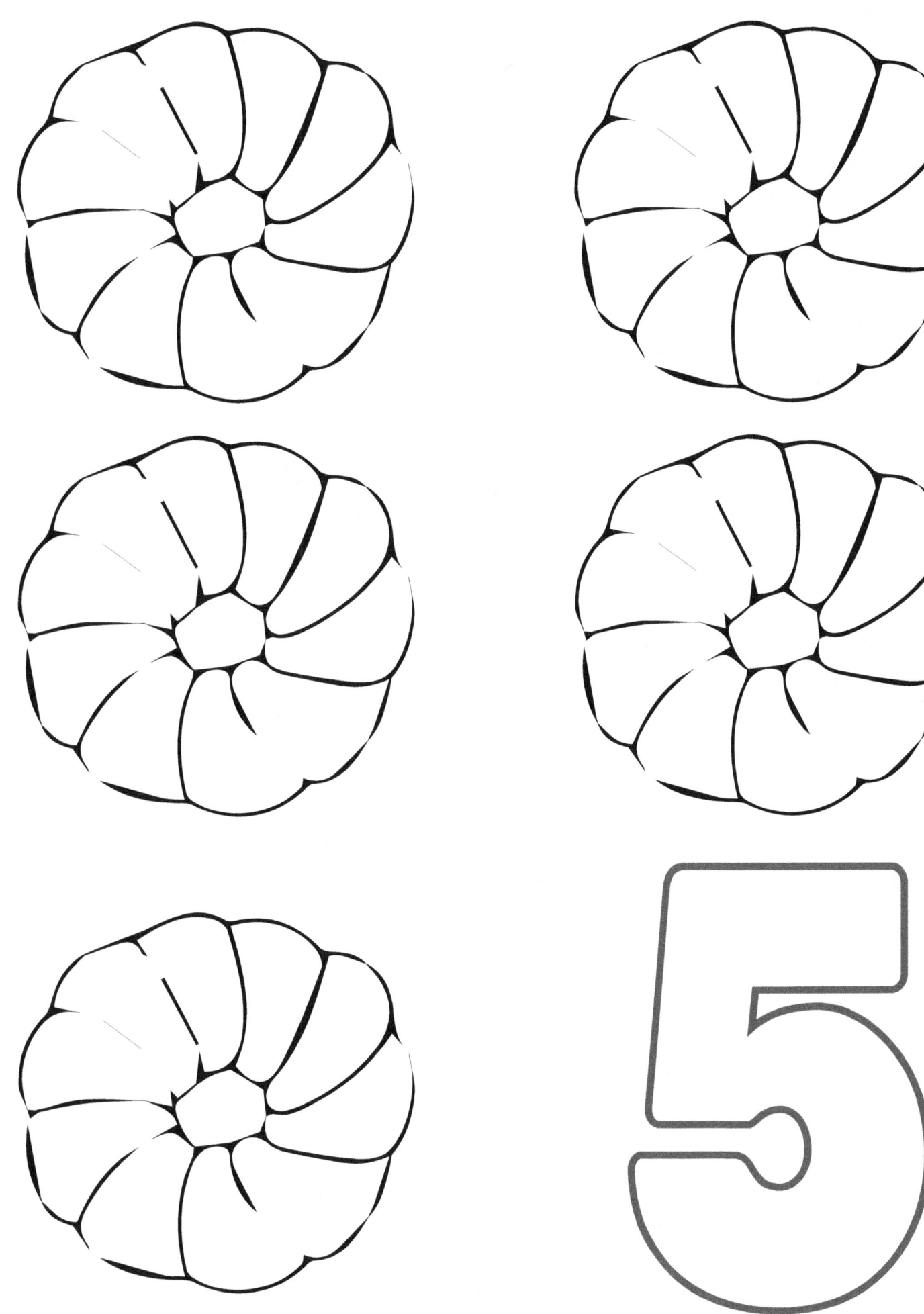

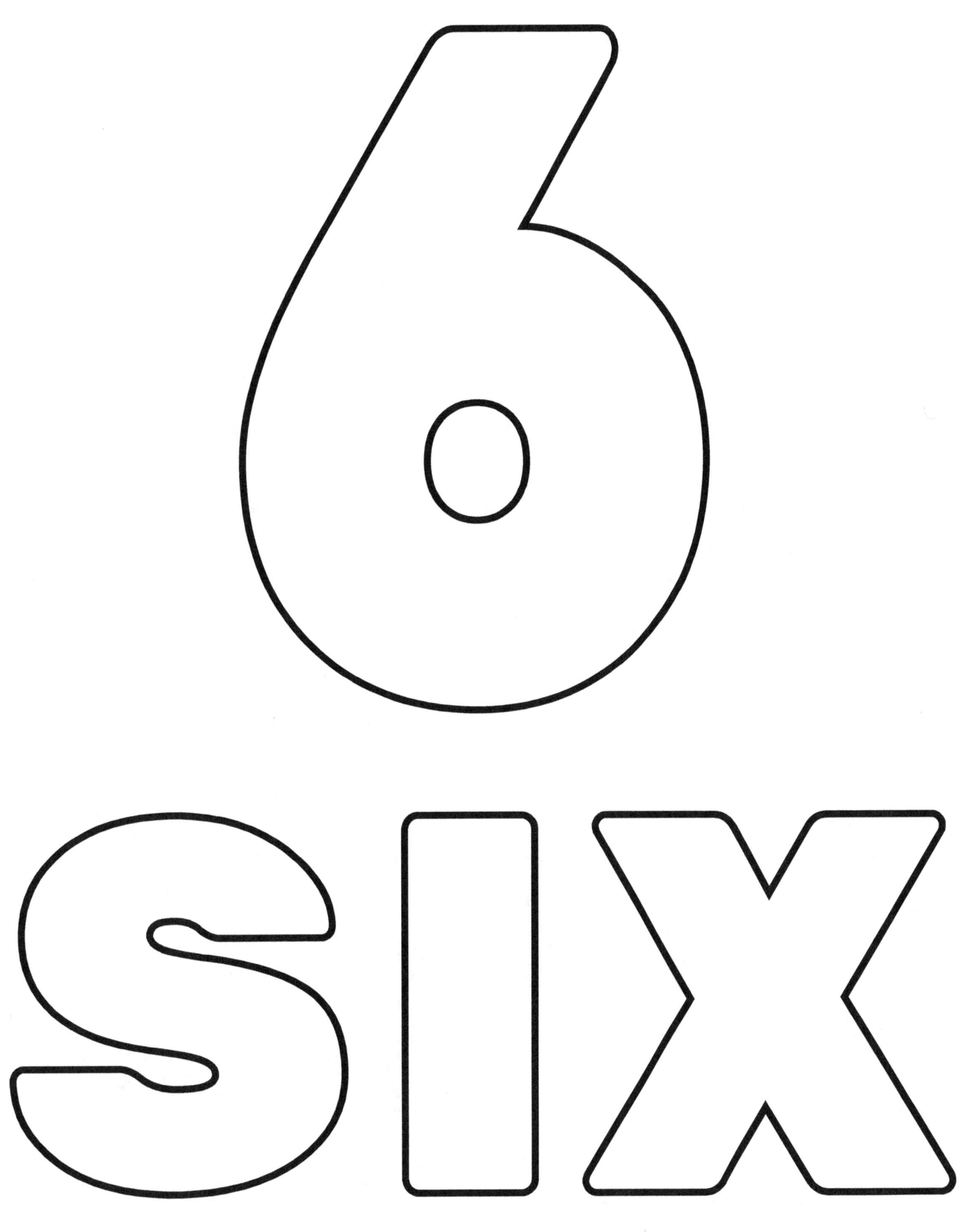

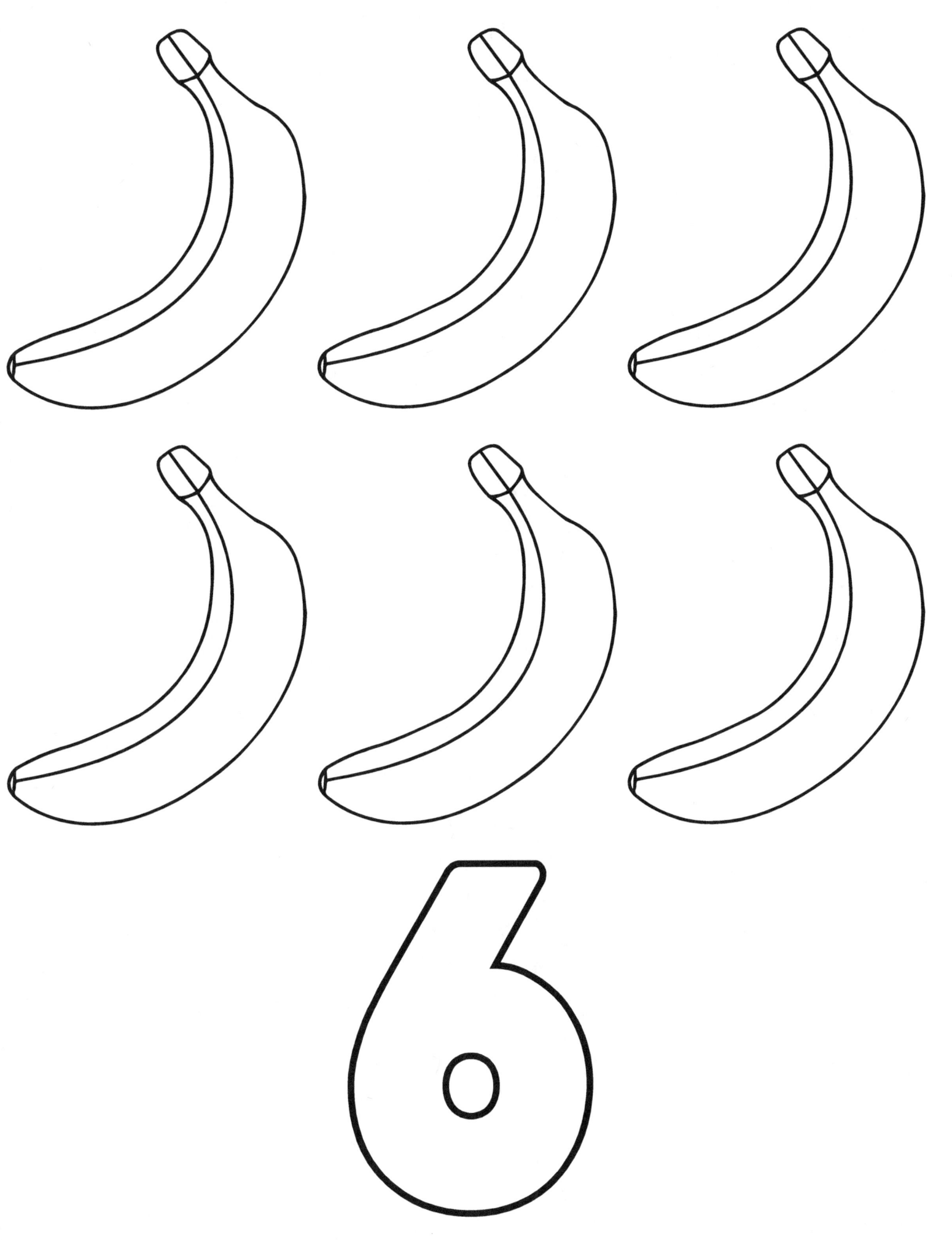

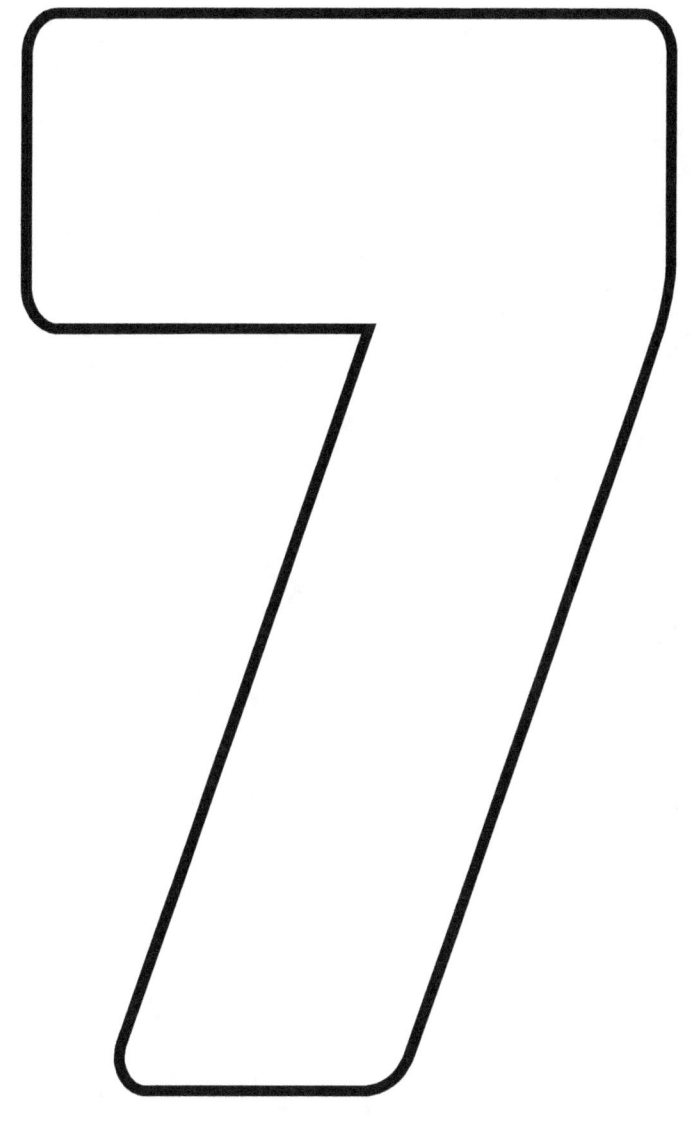

SEVEN

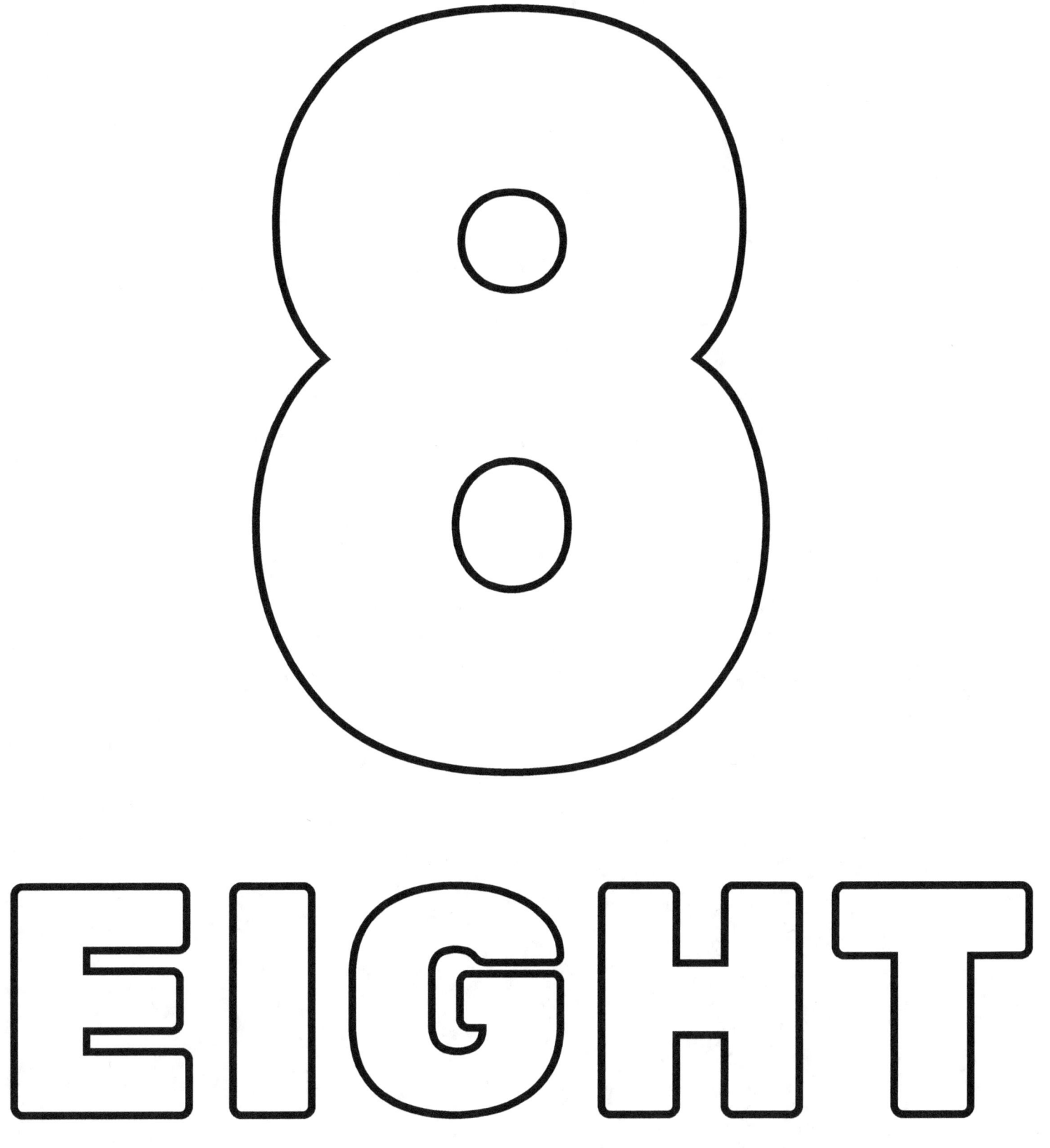

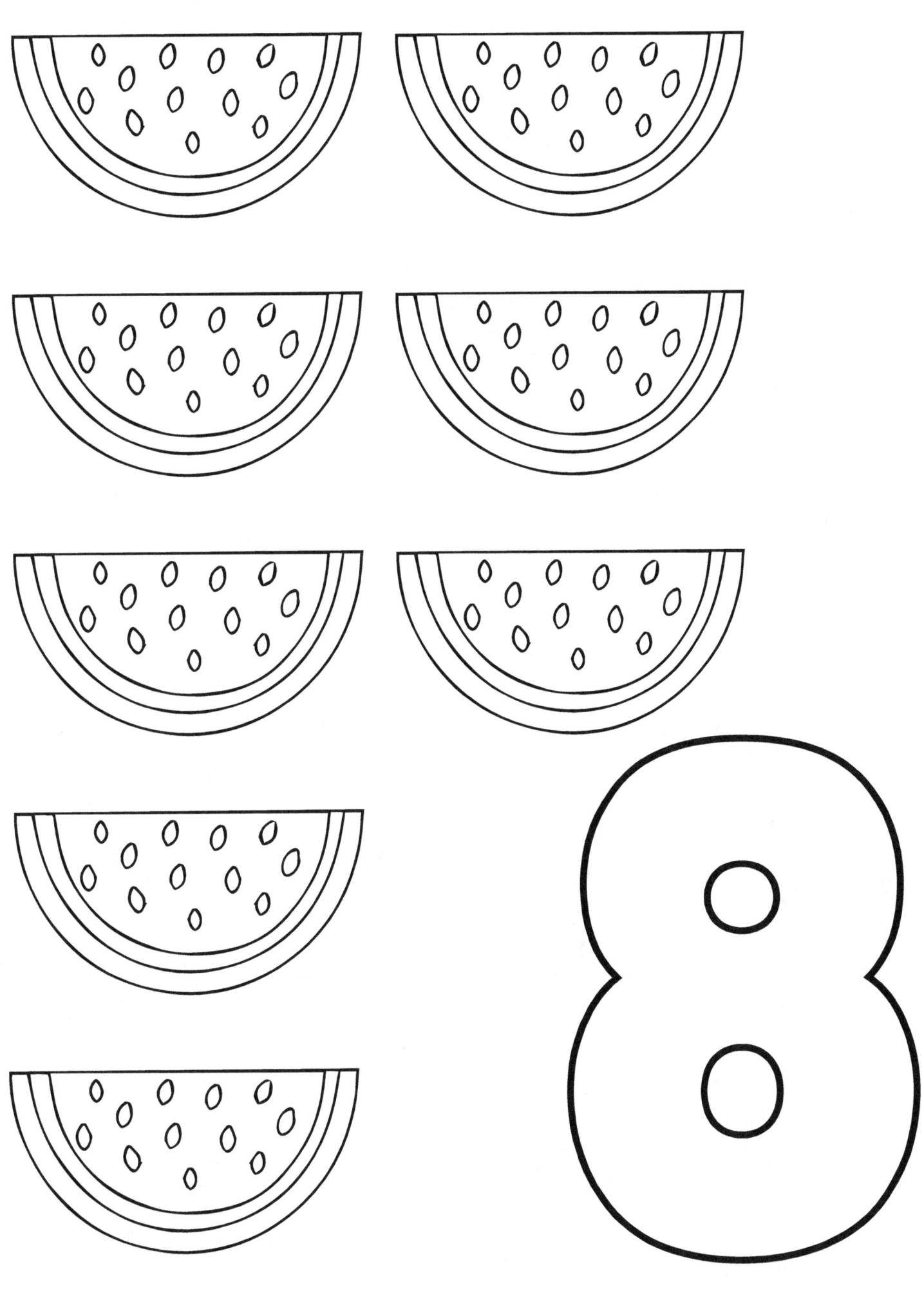

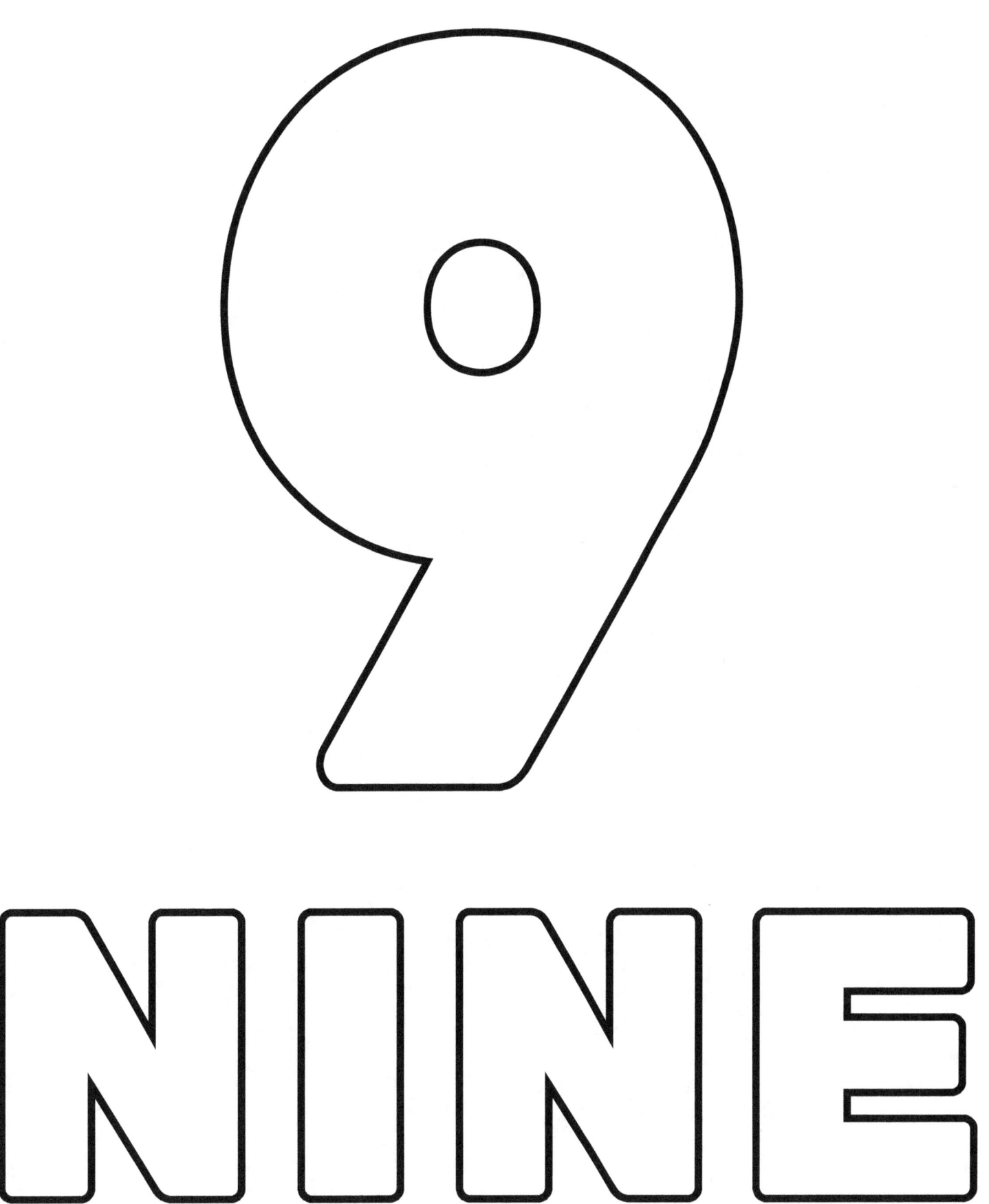

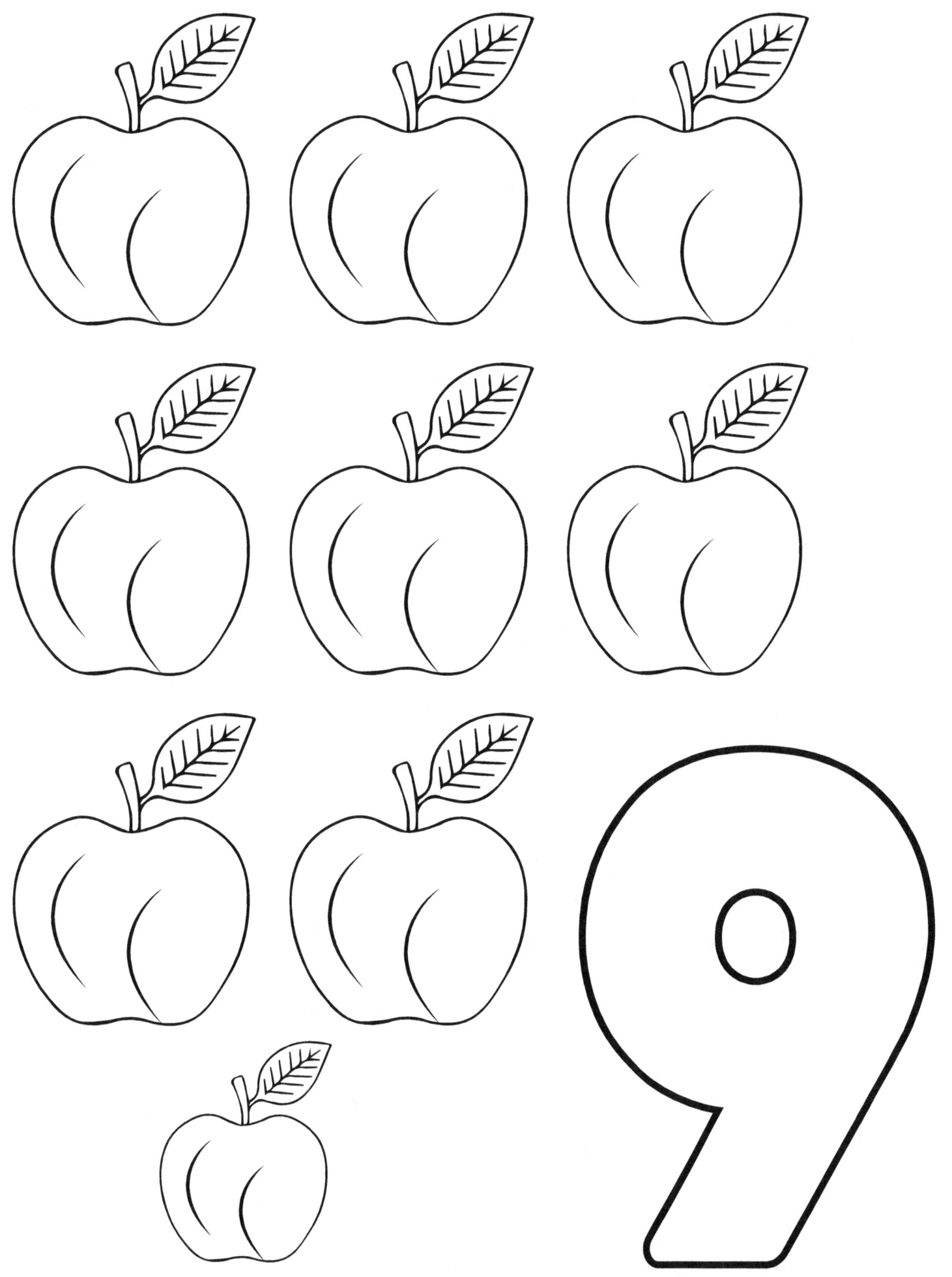

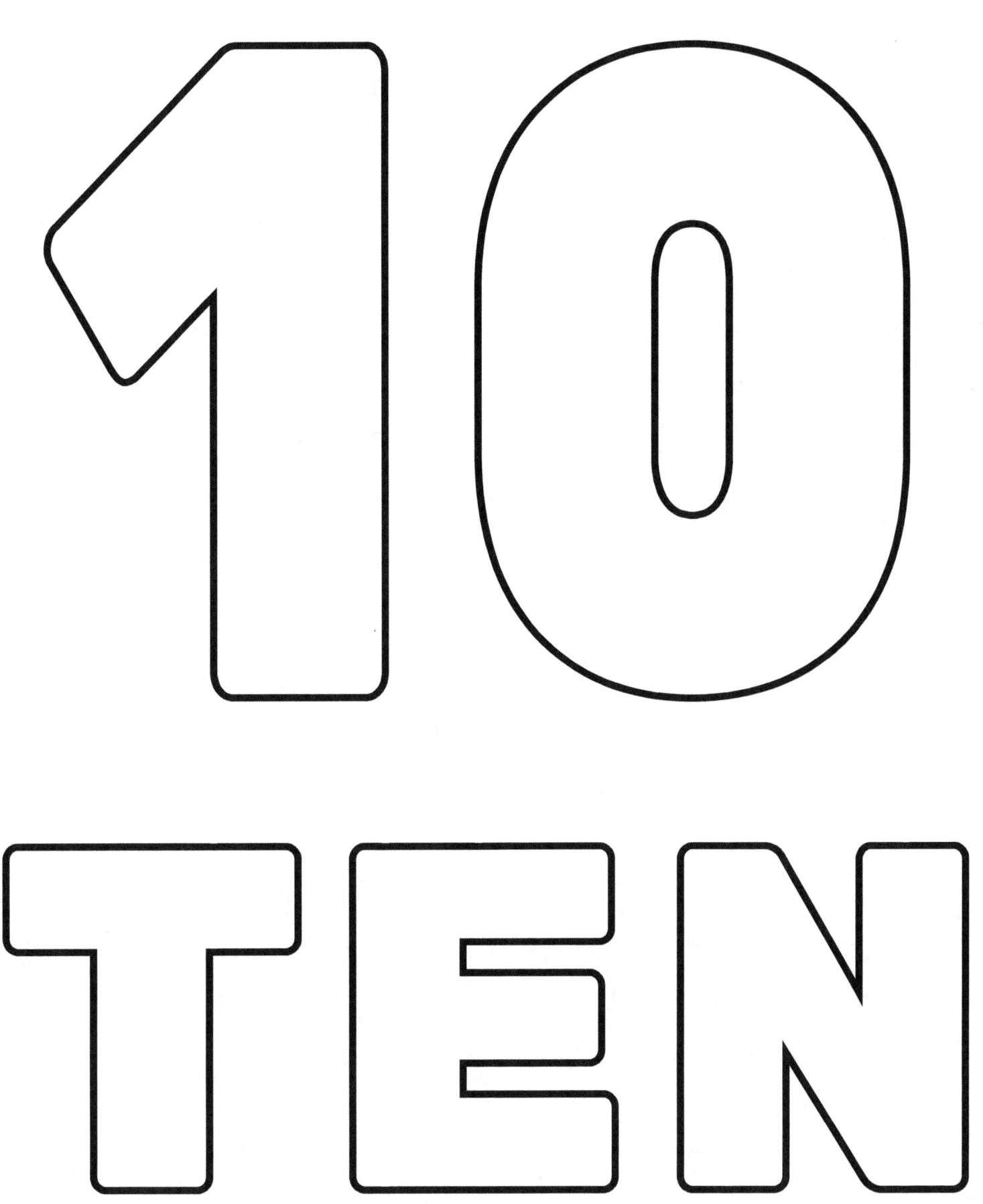

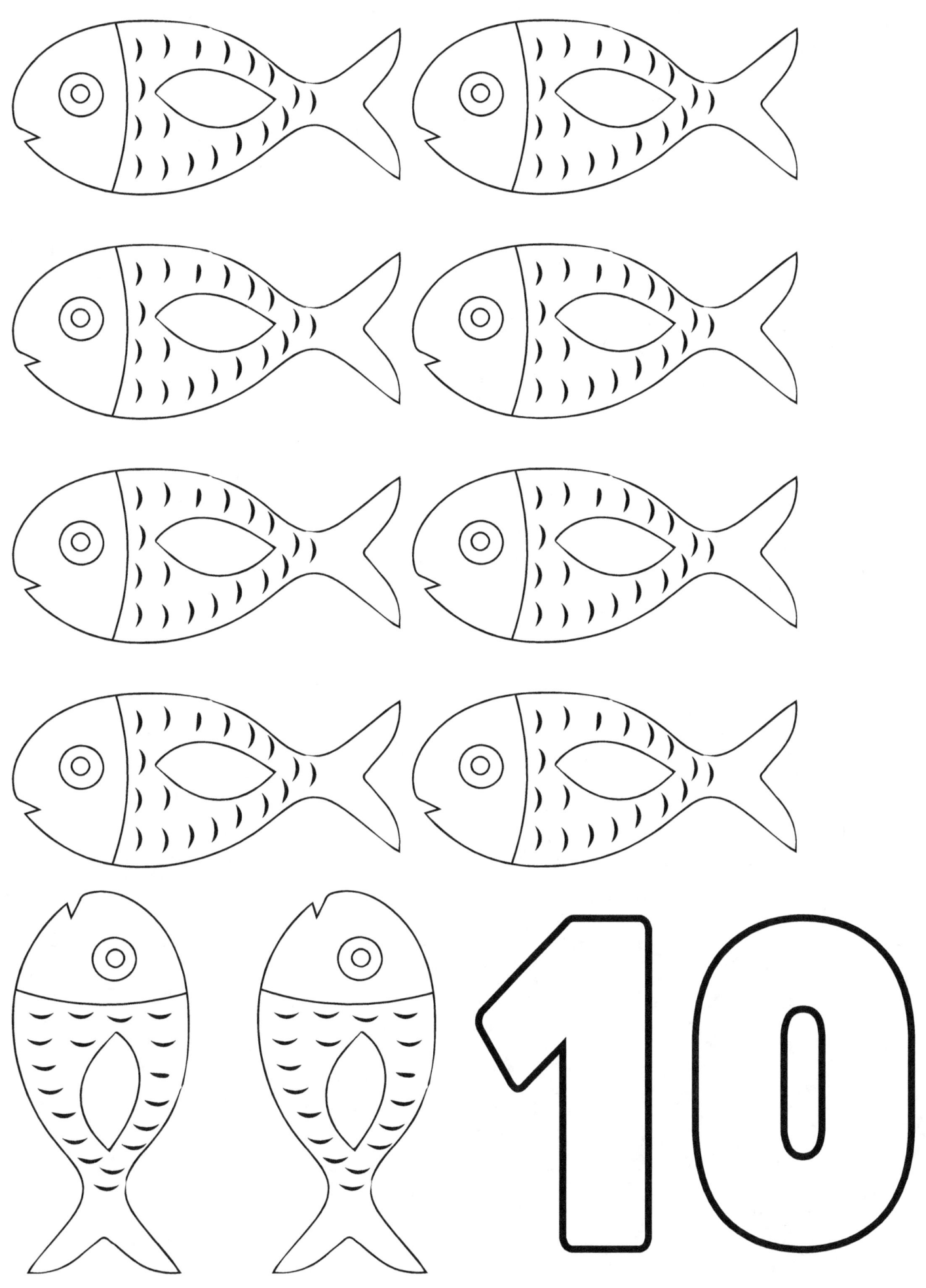

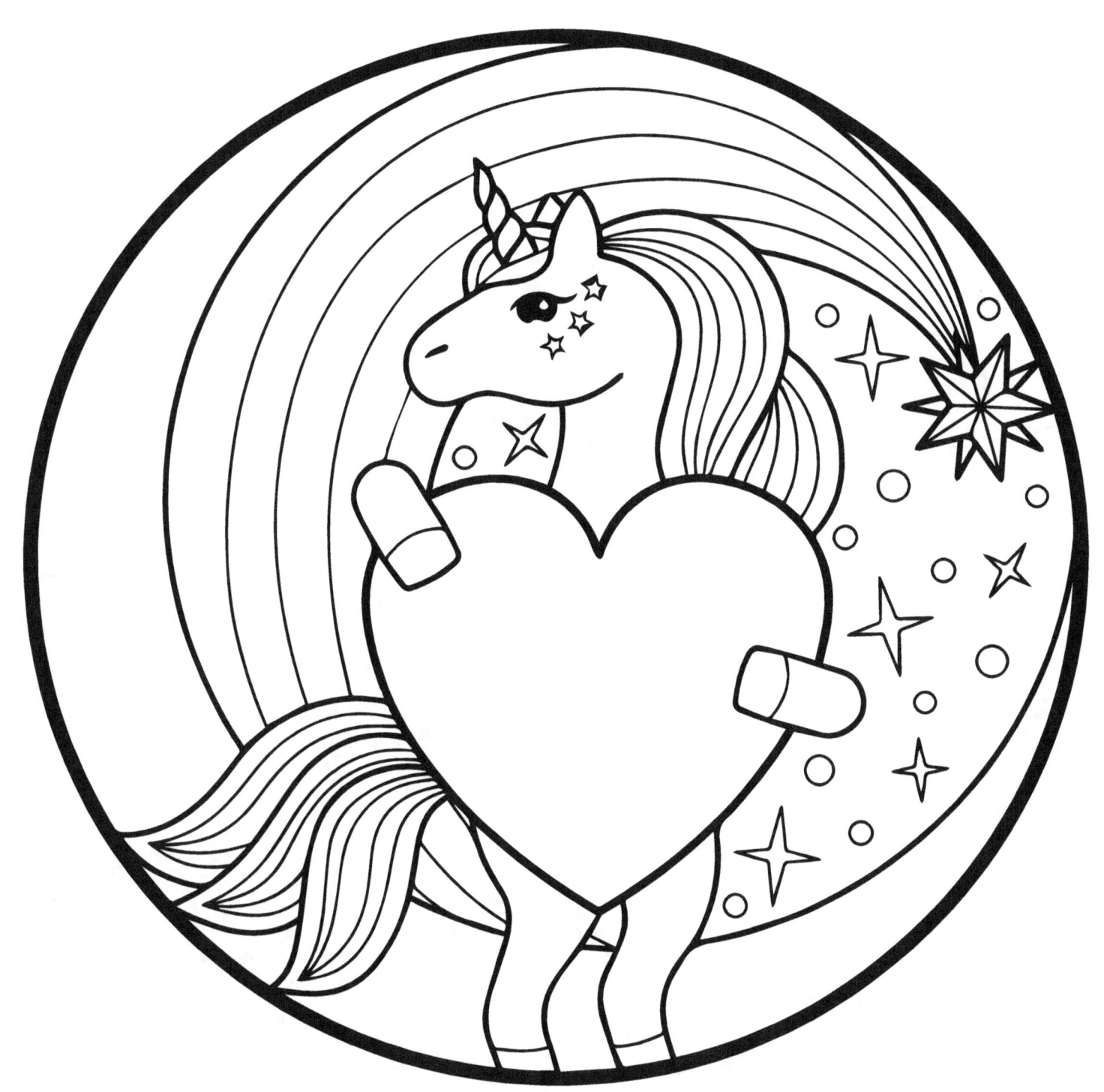

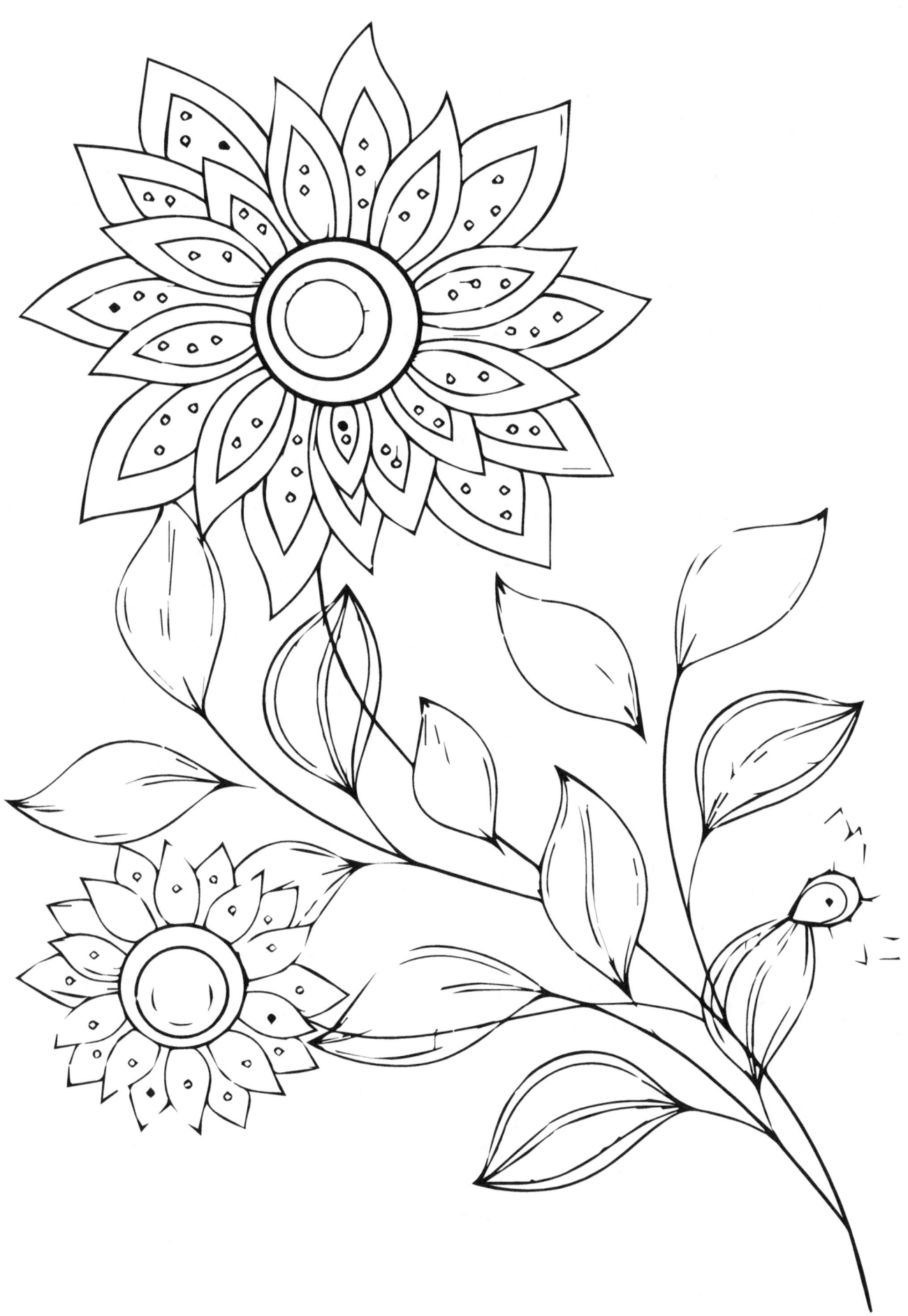

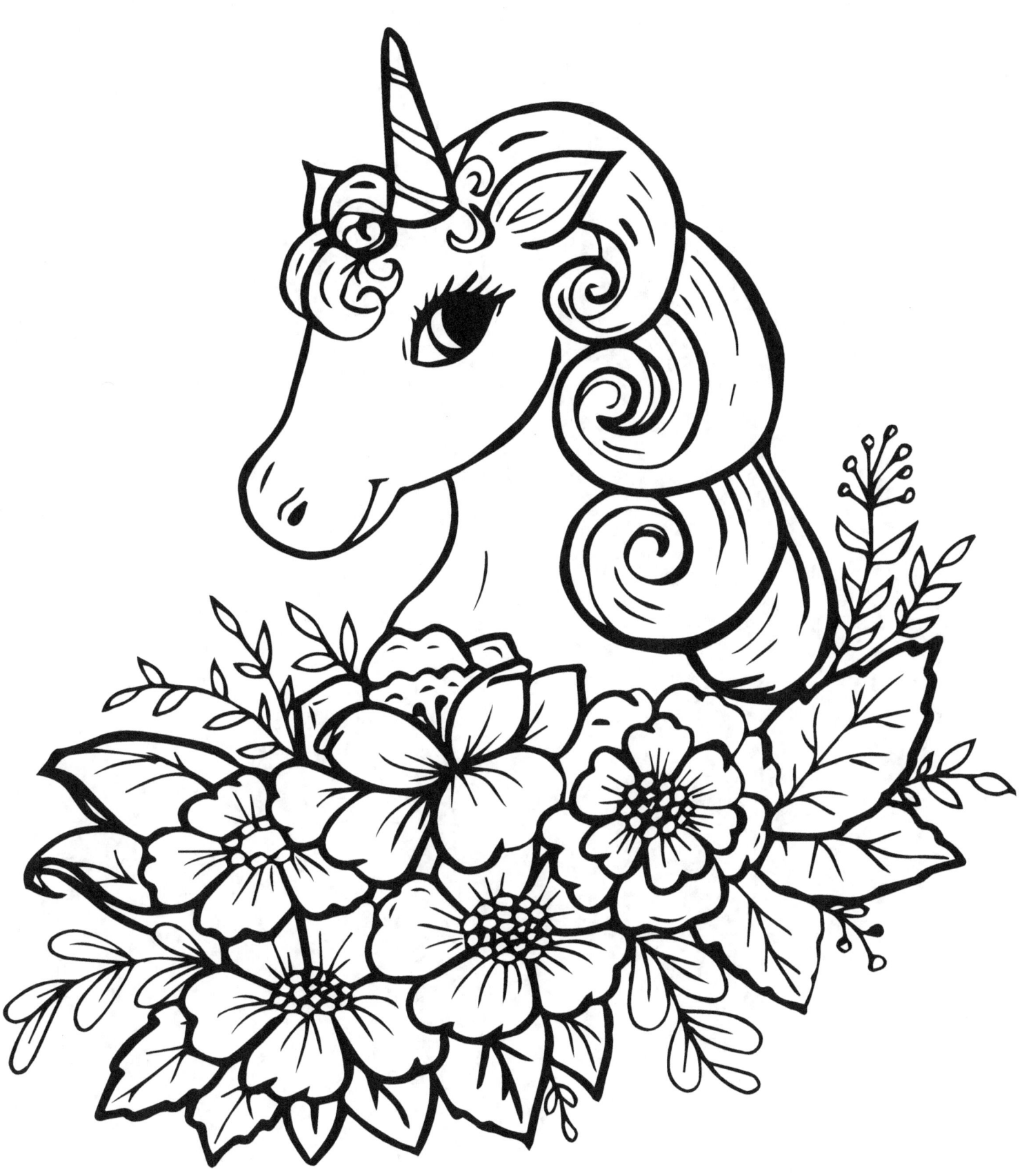

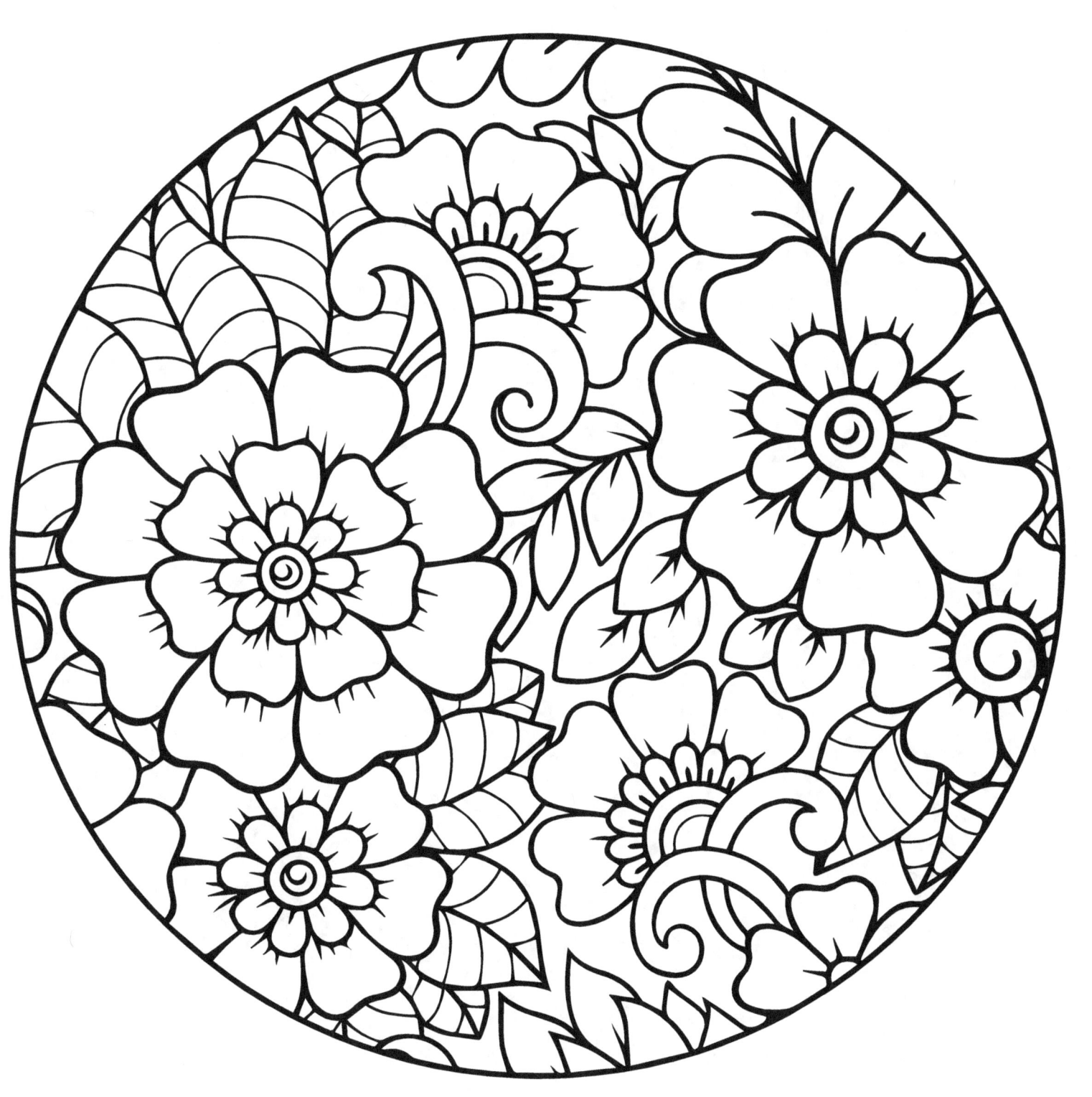

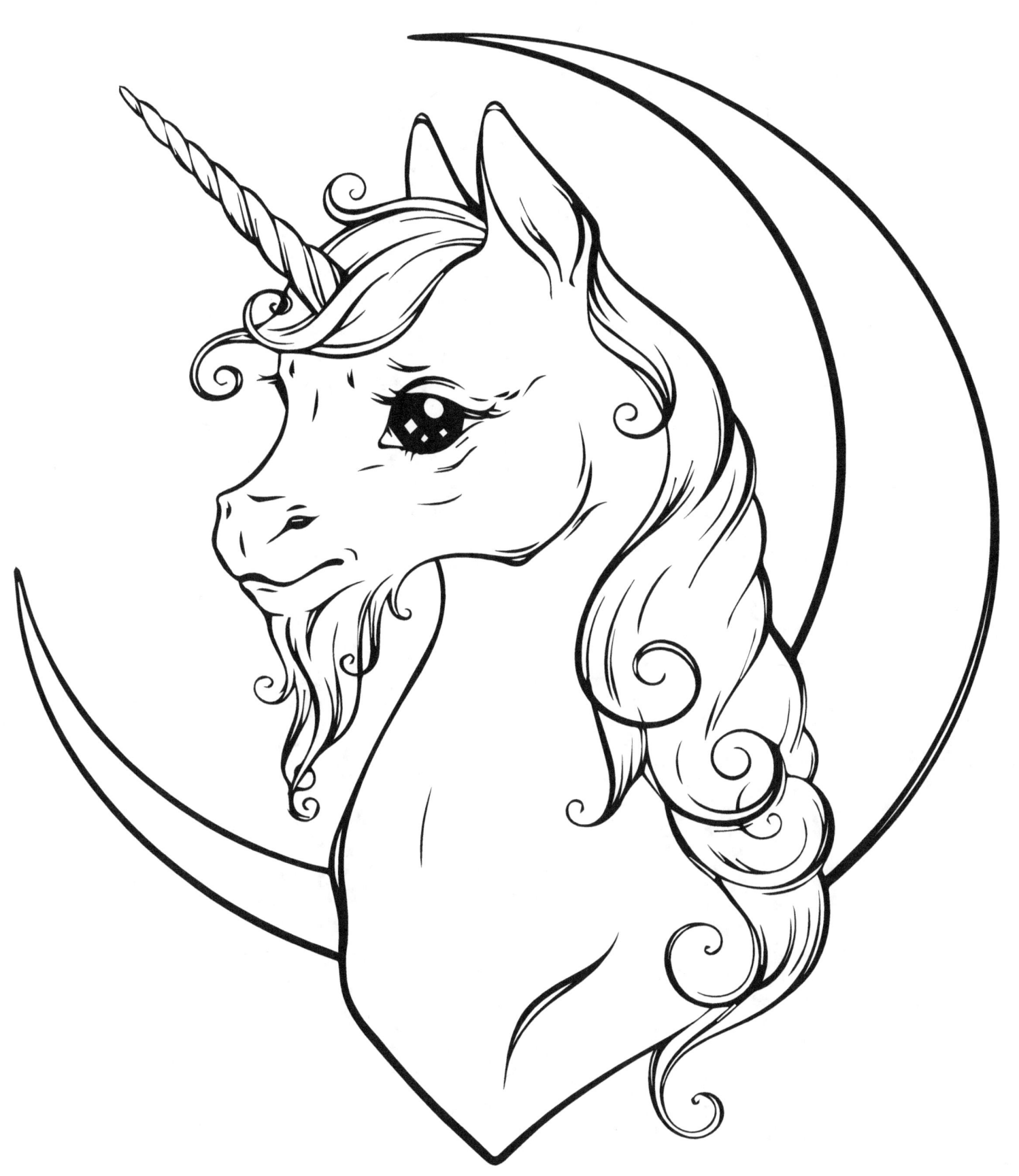

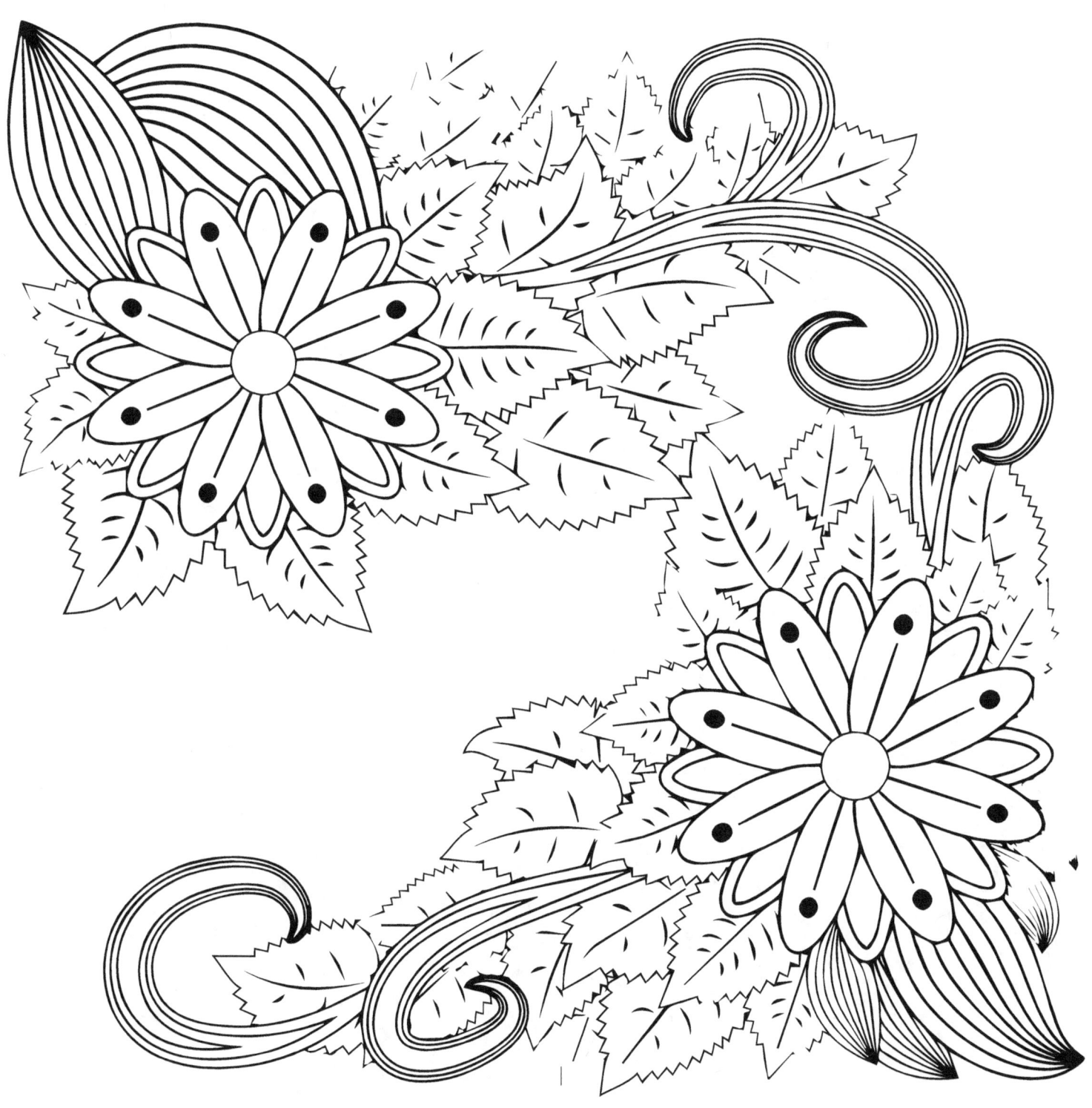

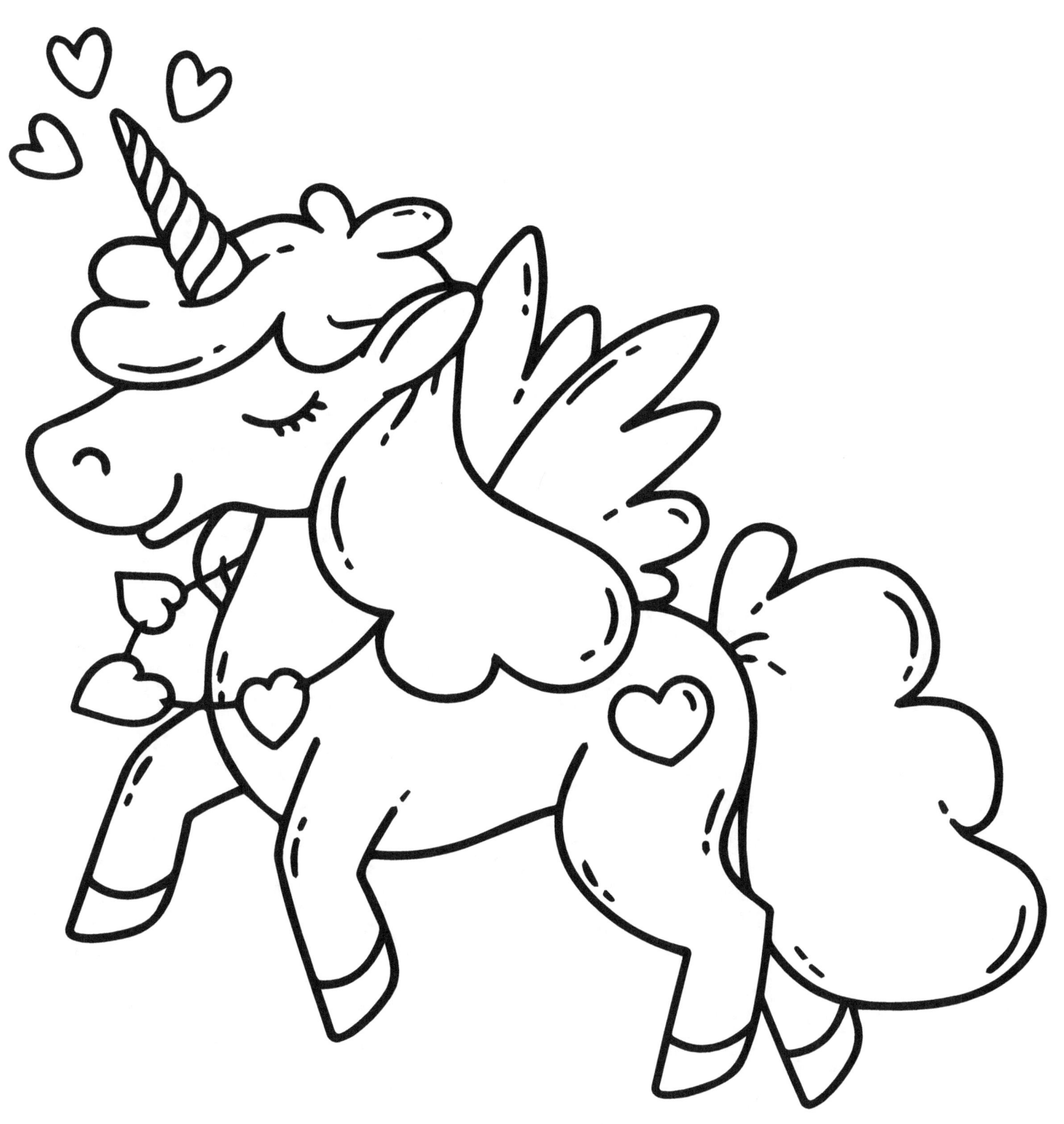

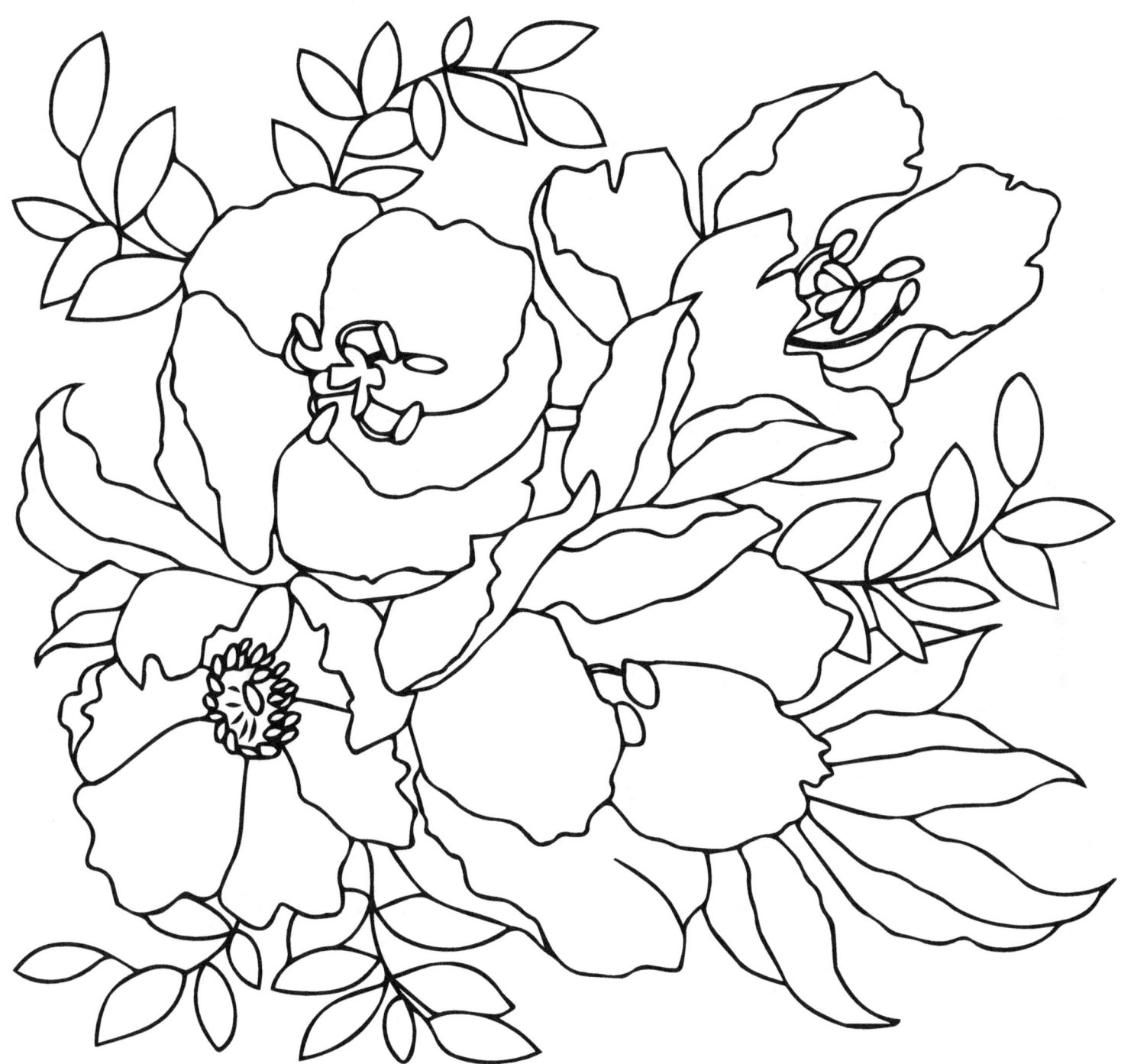

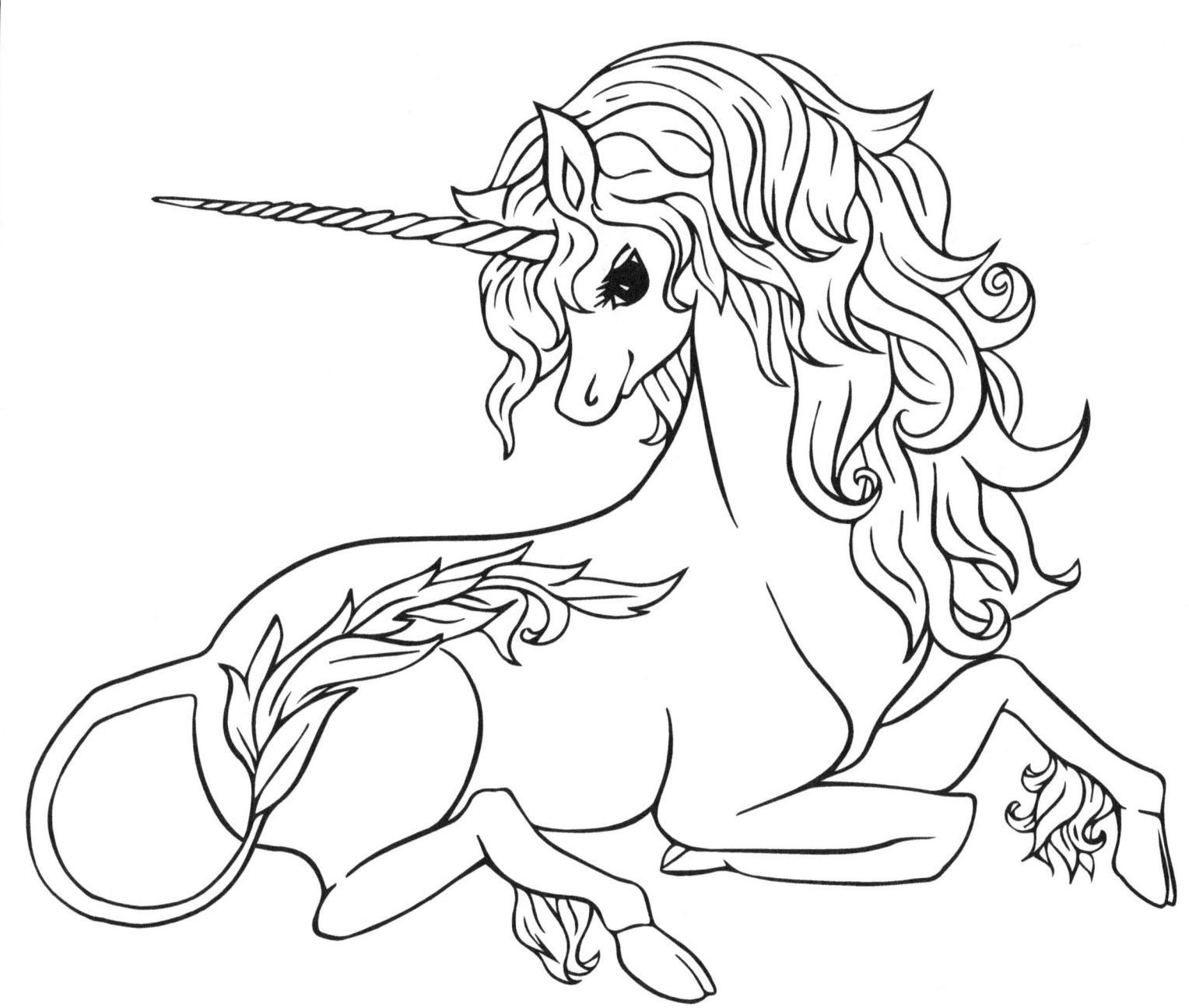

www.ingramcontent.com/pod-product-compliance
Lightning Source LLC
Chambersburg PA
CBHW081058240526

45465CB00025B/2688